TeamGuides
Pocket
Coach

T0358229

TeamGuides
Pocket
Coach

Brad Humphrey
Jeff Stokes

Jossey-Bass
Pfeiffer
San Francisco

Copyright © 1997 by Brad Humphrey and Jeff Stokes

ISBN:0–7879–1102–X

Library of Congress Cataloging-in-Publication Data

Humphrey, Brad, 1957–
    TeamGuides pocket coach / Brad Humphrey and Jeff Stokes.
      p. cm.
    ISBN 0–7879–1102–X (acid-free paper)
    1. Teams in the workplace. 2. Scheduling. 3. Decision-making,
  Group. 4. Customer services. 5. Industrial project management.
  I. Stokes, Jeff, 1957–   . II. Title. III. Title: Team guides
  pocket coach.
  HD66.H85 1997
  658.4'036—dc21   97–21102

Published by

350 Sansome Street, 5th Floor
San Francisco, California 94104–1342
(415) 433–1740; Fax (415) 433–0499
(800) 274–4434; Fax (800) 569–0443

Visit our website at: http://www.pfeiffer.com

Outside of the United States, Pfeiffer products can be purchased from the following Simon & Schuster International Offices:

Prentice Hall
Campus 400
Maylands Avenue
Hemel Hempstead
Hertfordshire HP2 7EZ
United Kingdom
44(0) 1442 881891; Fax 44(0) 1442 882074

Prentice Hall Professional
Locked Bag 507
Frenchs Forest PO NSW 2086
Australia
61 2 9454 2200; Fax 61 2 9453 0089

Simon & Schuster (Asia) Pte Ltd
317 Alexandra Road
#04–01 IKEA Building
Singapore 159965
Asia
65 476 4688; Fax 65 378 0370

Prentice Hall/Pfeiffer
P.O. Box 1636
Randburg 2125
South Africa
27 11 781 0780; Fax 27 11 781 0781

Printing 10   9   8   7   6   5   4   3   2   1

 This book is printed on acid-free, recycled stock that meets or exceeds the minimum GPO and EPA requirements for recycled paper.

Form Selection Guide

The forms in this "pocket coach" are arranged in the same order as in *TeamGuides*. The form name and number will be provided to promote greater compatibility between *TeamGuides* and *TeamGuides Pocket Coach*.

The four main sections of *TeamGuides* are presented below with the name of the forms associated with that section. Please note that the page numbers are for this book only and do not correspond to page numbers from *TeamGuides*.

Meeting-Management Forms

Problem-Solving Tools

Customer/Supplier-Relationship Tools

Project-Assessment Forms

Acknowledgments

Special thanks to Ty Cross, Ila Genova, Vickie Knight, and Ron Roberts, of Pinnacle Performance Group®, for assisting in the compilation of the forms and for contributing their creativity and ideas over the past years. Also, a special thanks should go to all of the clients of Pinnacle Performance Group® who offered special insights to the effectiveness of the forms and encouraged their use.

Brad Humphrey
Jeff Stokes
June 1997

About the Authors

Brad Humphrey and Jeff Stokes are the developers of *TeamGuides* and the authors of *TeamGuides Pocket Coach*. They are the co-founders of Pinnacle Performance Group®, a training and consulting firm dedicated to assisting organizations reposition themselves to be competitive, effective, and profitable. For information about Pinnacle Performance Group® or for training workshops on the *TeamGuides* please write to: Pinnacle Performance Group, 7011 Martindale, Shawnee, KS 66218.

Introduction

Purpose

The purpose of *TeamGuides* is to provide you with the right "paper tools" for better organization and performance results. Though a few of the forms have their origins in the quality movement, the majority of the forms are new and have been field tested for their use and effectiveness. Using *TeamGuides* will save you time and energy, thus allowing your efforts to be more effective, efficient, and profitable.

The *TeamGuides Pocket Coach* was written to support *TeamGuides* and serves as your personal "translator" or guide. This book provides expanded instructions for each form contained in *TeamGuides*. It explains the purpose and application of each form, all in a compact format.

If your organization has taken a formal approach to quality and continuous improvement, you have probably made the following observations:

1. Meetings now take up a greater portion of your workday than ever before.
2. You and your associates are involved in more problem solving, customer service, and decision making, often as a team.
3. Documenting meeting activities, decisions, problems, and so on, is a growing expectation from top management.

TeamGuides was created specifically to support these three observations and is divided into four sections: Meeting Management, Problem Solving, Customer/Supplier Relationship, and Project Assessment. Each section contains several "master" forms that can be photocopied and used to provide structure to whatever need you might have. A brief overview of the four sections of *TeamGuides*, which also represents what will be expanded upon in this book, follows.

Components

1. MEETING MANAGEMENT

Meetings continue to be the most practical option for bringing people together to discuss issues, solve problems, and make decisions. Effective meetings begin and end on time, are organized, produce a formal record of what was discussed, and provide direction for future activities.

The first section in *TeamGuides* represents the administrative side of meetings. The forms, or "paper tools," included in this section will help you organize each meeting, keep the meeting on task, record decisions and goals, and prepare action plans for executing needed tasks and goals.

2. PROBLEM SOLVING

Greater problem-solving and decision-making opportunities are being provided to employees. In the quest to be quality minded, be responsive to customers, and decrease operating expenses, organizations have realized that they need all employees to be involved with making their workplace more effective and efficient.

Whether working individually or as a team, a process is often followed to solve problems and make decisions. To complete a process step or to justify a decision, it is often important to document an observation, track an activity, or build on an idea. The second section of *TeamGuides* includes forms that offer structure to brainstorm, clarify, collect data, assess, and plan solutions.

3. CUSTOMER/SUPPLIER RELATIONSHIPS

Quality minded organizations realize that greater understanding of customers and suppliers is the key to success. This requires the identification of needs and requirements that can be measured and monitored.

The third section of *TeamGuides* contains four forms that can be used when working with internal or external customers and suppliers. *External customers* are those who pay for your firm's products or services. *External suppliers*, or vendors, are organizations that you pay for materials, services, or supplies.

Internal customers are individuals or departments that you send completed work to. *Internal suppliers* are the individuals or departments that you receive work from in order to complete your tasks. Within most organizations there are hundreds of internal customer/supplier relationships that must be maintained to better serve external customers.

4. PROJECT ASSESSMENT

Decisions are often based on benefits or savings associated with the decision. When benefits or savings must be expressed in financial terms, it is important to have the proper documentation.

The final section of *TeamGuides* includes several forms that quantify investment costs, expected savings, and return on investment (ROI). Whenever you need to justify expenditures, document your efforts using the forms contained in the fourth section of *TeamGuides*.

Using the *TeamGuides Pocket Coach*

Athletic coaches often use hand signals to communicate with their players during a game. Hand signals save time because they quickly relay messages and direction. To make the *TeamGuides Pocket Coach* easier to use, a few signals, or symbols, have been provided to make reading this book easier. A legend of the signals is provided below for your convenience.

PURPOSE

It is vital to know the purpose of each form. Some forms might have multiple uses and be helpful in more than one area. However, to ensure success, it is important to understand the best intended use of each form.

MODEL

Each form includes a completed form that demonstrates what the form should look like when completed. The model forms will have an administrative/service example for your reference.

CONSTRUCTION

The whistle symbol will point you toward the instructions to complete the form. You may want to have the appropriate form handy when you begin to complete it and use this section to guide you through the process.

COACHING TIPS

Before finalizing the form, it is wise to take a "time-out" and review your effort to ensure that you haven't forgotten anything. Additional coaching tips will also be included with each form.

Meeting-Management Forms

Meeting Outline FORM 1

Every scheduled meeting should have a written outline that
alerts individuals to what will be addressed at a meeting.

Meeting Outline

Meeting Logistics

TEAM/DEPARTMENT Data Processing   LOCATION Conference Room B

FACILITATOR Bob Johnson   DATE/TIME June 30, 9:00–10:00am

Meeting Purpose

Information giving

Focus: Identify specific programming needs of various departments.

Meeting Items

	TIME ALLOTTED
Review of current projects	9:00–9:05
Update on new software	9:05–9:15
Itemize programming requests	9:15–9:30
Discuss prioritization guidelines	9:30–9:45
Create next action step	9:45–9:55
Meeting wrap-up	9:55–10:00

Meeting Materials

	PERSON RESPONSIBLE
Departmental requests for programming	Julie B.
Status report on current projects (percent complete)	Tim L.
Comments and review of new software	Gary T.

MEETING OUTLINE

The Meeting Outline form is an administrative tool for meetings that provides direction, topics, and time restraints. It encourages meeting members to stick to a preset order of topics, thus reducing the amount of random discussion that often takes place in unorganized meetings.

To complete this form, follow the instructions listed below:

1. First, in the "Meeting Logistics" section, identify what group or team is to be included in this meeting. List individual names if meeting involves people from different areas. Full names or initials are acceptable.
2. Identify the facilitator or meeting leader by name.
3. Record meeting location, date, and time. Be sure to use actual room names or numbers to reduce confusion.
4. Briefly describe the purpose of the meeting in the "Meeting Purpose" section. Use the following purpose descriptions to assist your effort:

   - *Information giving* (IG) is a meeting in which information is provided to those in attendance.
   - *Information exchanging* (IE) is a meeting in which information is provided and an exchange is both allowed and warranted. Time for questions and discussion should be built into the meeting agenda.
   - *Information creating* (IC) is a meeting in which a formal brainstorming effort will be expected.

5. As you identify the purpose for the meeting, be sure to include what topic, or topics, will be the focus of the meeting. You may find it helpful to actually use the word *focus* in your description.
6. List the items to be addressed, in the proper order, under the "Meeting Items" section. It is wise to also include the time that will be allowed for each topic. Keep in mind that the time allowance can be an estimate that may need to be flexible, depending on the progress of the meeting.

7. Identify any resources, information, tools, and so on, that need to be in the meeting and list those items in the final section called "Meeting Materials."

TIP #1: Distribute completed agenda to meeting members at least two to five days before the meeting.

TIP #2: Before the meeting, make sure the meeting room is clean and has the needed supplies, such as markers, flip chart, table, and chairs.

TIP #3: If your company has a master meeting schedule, be sure to comply with scheduling guidelines or rules.

TIP #4: Begin the meeting by reviewing the agenda and remind everyone to respect the time allowance.

TIP #5: If agenda items change during the meeting, be sure to identify what was not addressed and when members would prefer to see them addressed.

Meeting Review FORM 2

A written summary of meeting discussions, decisions made, and assigned tasks should be made after each meeting.

Meeting Review

TEAM/DEPARTMENT	Data Processing	SCHEDULED TIME	9:00–10:00am
DATE	June 30	ACTUAL TIME	9:15–10:30am

Meeting Participants

Bob Johnson	Tim Layden	Theresa Smith	
Julie Babcock	Gary Timmons		

Subjects Discussed

Quick review of current projects. All projects progressing on schedule.

New software was discussed. So far all seems to be working well, no complaints from users.

Decided to form task force to prioritize programming requests. Group would consist of
one member from each department, plus vice president of Operations.

The task force would also create document that would provide guidelines for prioritization
and then distribute to all departments.

Who	What	Due Date
Julie	Facilitate meeting of department representatives	July 6
Tim	Prepare report on new software	July 8
Theresa	Create Prioritization Form	July 6

Parking Lot

Color laser printer purchase

Network update

MEETING REVIEW

The Meeting Review form is critical for recording meeting notes. Without a documented review, important points will be forgotten or misrepresented. This form will bring respect and credibility to the meeting and reinforce each member's accountability to what was discussed.

To complete this form, the meeting recorder should follow the instructions listed below:

1. Summarize the discussion points under the "Subjects Discussed" section on the form. (Do not try to record each word spoken.)
2. Record important comments and include the name of the individuals who made the comments. Such information will add to everyone's memory later.
3. When tasks or responsibilities are assigned, record who is performing the task, what the task is, and the due date for completing the task.
4. Write any topic or issue that is not part of the meeting agenda in the "Parking Lot" section. This section is for recording spontaneous comments so that meeting members will remember them.

TIP #1: Distribute cleaned-up copies of the Meeting Review to the meeting participants within one to two days.

TIP #2: Attach copies of handouts, graphs, charts, and any other materials that were part of meeting to the Meeting Review form.

TIP #3: Review "Parking Lot" issues periodically. Some of the items listed in that section often become future agenda items.

TIP #4: Distribute blank copies of the Meeting Review form to meeting participants to allow them to take their own notes. This is a subtle way to develop meeting recorders.

TIP #5: Keep a copy of each meeting's Meeting Review form on file for future reference.

TIP #6: Read aloud the previous meeting's Meeting Review at the beginning of the meeting. This serves to refresh everyone's memory.

Goals List FORM 3

Departments and work teams often create goals to improve the organization, a department, a work function, and so on. This form allows a list of such goals to be kept for constant attention and review.

Goals List

TEAM/DEPARTMENT __Customer Service__   DATE __June 5__

Goals

1. _Cut response time to customer calls 15% by January 1._

2. _Increase overall customer satisfaction rating on surveys to 95% in next nine months._

3. _Provide conflict resolution training to all Customer Service reps by end of year._

4. _Present Customer Service mission and vision to all other departments before January 1._

5. _____

6. _____

7. _____

GOALS LIST

Developing goals is very important to organizations. Often, departments and/or teams are required to set goals for future achievement. This form allows team members to list their goals so that there is less chance of any goal being forgotten.

To complete this form, follow the sequence listed below:

1. First identify the department or team by name and the date the form is first used.
2. The leader of the department or team should record each goal as it is developed by the department or team.
3. Date each goal as it is achieved.

TIP #1: Keep this form posted in a visible area so that members involved with the goal process can see it.

TIP #2: Use the Goals List at meetings to remind people of goals and to solicit update information.

TIP #3: As goals are achieved, recognize and /or reward the team members.

Goal Worksheet FORM 4

Each goal that the team develops needs to have an action plan. This form allows the team to record the "who, what, and when" associated with each step to fulfill the goal.

Goal Worksheet

TEAM/DEPARTMENT Customer Service   DATE June 12

Goal

Provide conflict-resolution training to all Customer Service reps by end of the year.

Objective

#	DATE	RESPONSIBLE	ASSIGNED TASK
1	6/18	Department	Determine specific topics for training sessions
2	6/25	John W. & Brad J.	Assemble list of training firms/companies
3	7/2	Jane B. & Ronnie H.	Define budget requirements for training
4	7/9	Lloyd N. & Curt R.	Secure training company
5	7/16	Jim N. & Ed G.	Create final list of all employees to receive training
6	7/23	Bob, Brad, Lloyd, & Ed	Divide Customer Service reps into training groups
7	7/30	Jane, Ronnie, & John	Create training schedule
8	8/15	Department	Begin training

GOALS WORKSHEET

Developing a Goal Worksheet for each goal will clarify the team's purpose, provide confidence in the outcome of the goal, and assure accountability. It should be completed and given to each individual involved in the goal process.

To complete this form, follow the sequence listed below:

1. Identify what department or team is involved with the goal.
2. Record the date when the worksheet is completed.
3. Record the actual goal statement in its entirety. (The statement should be same as the statement listed on the Goals List form.)
4. For each step, identify who is involved, what action the individual will take, and when the action step is to be completed (approximate date).

TIP #1: Keep this form posted in a visible area so that members involved with goal process can see it.

TIP #2: Use the Goal Worksheet at meetings to remind people of the goals and solicit update information.

TIP #3: Distribute a copy of the form to all involved parties.

TIP #4: Have a department or team member act as sponsor for the goal process. The person or department will be responsible for helping the team to achieve its goal and will provide updates to the team and those outside the team whenever appropriate.

TIP #5: Keep a copy of the Goal Worksheet on file for future reference.

TIP #6: Attach other supporting documentation, such as charts, graphs, or articles, to the Goal Worksheet form when necessary.

Team Charter FORM 5

This form provides a formal overview of any newly created team. The team's charter can include its membership, purpose, sponsorship, needs, objectives, meeting schedule, or anticipated budget needs.

Team Charter

TEAM NAME	Customer Service
TEAM RECORDER	Cheryl Miller
TEAM FACILITATOR(S)	Bonnie Johnson
TEAM SPONSOR(S)	Jack Jordan
PROPOSED TEAM MEMBERS	Dick Epsy, Jan Jones, Mike Bellick, Jerry Upshaw, Scott Hamilton

Problem/Topic Statement

Paper waste is approximately 3–5% more than is acceptable.

Current Impact of Problem/Topic

Increased paper costs are decreasing budget allowances for other office items.

WE WERE BROUGHT TOGETHER TO

Accurately cost-out the paper waste. Recommend methods to reduce paper usage within the Accounting and Sales departments.

PROBLEM-SOLVING TOOLS TO BE USED

Cause and Effect Chart, Cost Benefit Analysis, Check Sheet, Customer Needs Analysis, Pareto Chart

Customers Impacted

Possibly all because prices might decrease if we reduce paper costs.

Suppliers Impacted

Current paper suppliers—reduced paper needs would reflect less volume supplied by outside vendors.

MEETINGS

FREQUENCY 2 meetings/month   DAYS Thursday   LENGTH 1 hour

ANTICIPATED BUDGET NEEDS

Unsure—Employee time to meet

SIGN OFF Jerry Kramer   CHARTER GRANT DATE July 18

TEAM CHARTER

The Team Charter keeps people informed as to who is on what team and what is the team's objective. The form should be completed before a team begins its task, and the team should give the form to the appropriate senior leadership for approval. Without a chartering process, different teams may form and begin working on the *same* improvement opportunities. The Team Charter form allows senior management to monitor workplace teams and their focus and to make sure individuals are not overextending themselves by serving on too many teams.

To complete this form, follow the sequence listed below:

1. Record the name of the team if known. If unknown, add the name to the charter at a later time.
2. Identify the team leader, including the team facilitator, team recorder, and team sponsor.
3. List the names of all proposed team members.
4. Define the problem or topic that the team will be addressing in the section titled "Problem/Topic Statement."
5. Describe the current impact of the problem or topic on work performance, people, or processes.
6. Describe why this team was brought together and what is the team's ultimate goal. (An actual goal statement can used.)
7. List any problem-solving tools. (See section 3, Problem-Solving Tools, for resources that may be used.)
8. If there is an anticipated impact on customers or suppliers, describe what impact may be made.
9. In the "Meetings" section, list all scheduling information that is known.
10. In the "Anticipated Budget Needs" section, include an estimate of the costs involved with the team's effort. Costs should consider labor, meeting supplies, resources, trips, and so on.
11. Senior management will fill in the "Sign Off" and "Charter Date" sections.

TIP #1: If possible, complete the Team Charter before beginning any team activity.

TIP #2: Make sure you have a sponsor that will invest his or her time and interest into the team.

TIP #3: Be sure that the senior managers responsible for the team members have copies of the charter to help keep them informed.

TIP #4: Keep a copy of the Team Charter in the team's files or note-book. Periodically, have the team members reflect on the charter to see if they are complying with its initial direction and objectives.

TIP #5: As a team, be prepared to update appropriate senior managers about the team's progress on a monthly or quarterly basis.

Team Progress Report FORM 6

The Team Progress Report should be used when a work team needs to keep senior management posted on the team's progress on a particular project.

Team Progress Report

TEAM _Phone Callers_

RECOGNIZE TEAM'S ACCOMPLISHMENT	
(DATE) _May 15_	
TRACK MONITORING SYSTEM (DATE) _May 6_	
Think Beyond the Fix	
Get Feedback	
IMPLEMENT CORRECTIVE ACTION PLAN	
(DATE) _April 28_	
PERT Chart	
Anticipate Potential Problems	
Present to Management	
DEVELOP LONG-TERM CORRECTIVE ACTION	
(DATE) _April 21_	
Make Decisions Based on Consensus	
Evaluate Alternative Solutions	
Brainstorm Potential Solutions	
Analyze Possible Causes	
Review Gathered Data	
BRAINSTORM AND TEST CAUSES	
(DATE) _April 14_	
Verify Causes	
Identify Causes	
Implement Interim Corrective Action (Band-Aid)	
DEFINE THE PROBLEM (DATE) _April 4_	
Problem Selection	
Problem Identification	
PROJECT STARTED (DATE) _April 1_	

Problem/Goal

New voice mail
communication
system is not
consistently recording
and saving messages
properly.

TEAM PROGRESS REPORT

The Team Progress Report allows a team that is responsible for solving a problem to show its progress to senior management. To do this, the "thermometer" should be colored up to the individual step that the team has completed. This form will hold the team accountable for completing its project and also keep others posted on the group's progress.

To complete this form, follow the sequence listed below:

1. Record the name of the department or team involved with the project.
2. Record the problem statement in the "Problem/Goal" section.
3. Record the team's goal statement in the "Problem/Goal" section.
4. Write in the date the project started and color in the first circle at the bottom of the thermometer.
5. Proceed to color the areas of the thermometer as the team completes the different steps. Be sure to write in the date that each step was completed.

TIP #1: Keep this form posted in a visible area so that members of the team can see it.

TIP #2: Include this form at meetings to remind people of progress made to date.

TIP #3: The thermometer provides a graphic that is easy for most individuals to understand. Keep it posted and updated regularly.

Meeting Evaluation FORM 7

Meetings must be productive, and this form allows team members to measure a meeting's level of effectiveness.

Meeting Evaluation

TEAM/DEPARTMENT   Purchasing   DATE   April 26
FACILITATOR   Charles Porter   TIME   11:00

CIRCLE ONE OF THE FOLLOWING NUMBERS FOR EACH QUESTION

1. THE MEETING OBJECTIVES WERE . . .
1　2　3　(4)　5
UNCLEAR　　　　　VERY CLEAR

2. THE MEETING TIME WAS USED . . .
1　2　3　4　(5)
POORLY　　　　　WELL

3. PARTICIPANTS EXPRESSED THEIR VIEWS . . .
1　2　(3)　4　5
CAUTIOUSLY　　　　OPENLY

4. THE GROUP WORKED TOGETHER . . .
1　2　3　(4)　5
POORLY　　　　EXCELLENTLY

5. IMPROVEMENT IN OUR TEAM/DEPARTMENT IS . . .
1　2　3　(4)　5
POOR　　　　EXCELLENT

Positive Comments

We stuck to the agenda and didn't get off the subject. We started the meeting on time and
ended on time. We didn't try to do too much at once, either.

Improvement Opportunities

Need more participation from everyone—some people were holding
back their ideas and opinions.

MEETING EVALUATION

Time is a precious commodity in most organizations. Therefore, meetings should provide optimum value to those in attendance. The Meeting Evaluation form provides a feedback system for the team to ensure that its meetings are productive and timely.

To complete this form, follow the sequence listed below:

1. Complete the needed information in the four sections: "Team/Department," "Facilitator," "Date," and "Time."
2. Read each of the five statements before you rank them. The statements reflect five different areas of a meeting.
3. Rank each of the five statements by circling the appropriate number. Notice that "1" indicates a low rating and "5" represents a high rating.
4. Record any positive observations about the meeting in the "Positive Comments" section.
5. List any areas needing attention and/or improvement in the "Improvement Opportunities" section.

TIP #1: Have members complete the Meeting Evaluation form after every fourth meeting for the first 90 days and thereafter once every eight to ten meetings.

TIP #2: Always compile total responses from the evaluations and make the information available to the members.

TIP #3: Address any negative trend or comments with the team and ask for input on how to improve the problem.

TIP #4: Give the evaluation at the conclusion of a regularly scheduled meeting and have all members complete the form before returning to their own work area.

TIP #5: Provide the compiled results to the appropriate senior manager.

Problem-Solving Tools

.

Brainstorming FORM 8

When it is critical to generate new ideas, the Brainstorming form provides a written record of what was brainstormed during the meeting and the name of the individual who provided the idea.

Brainstorming

Situation

The Sales and Customer Service departments are getting different data on product delivery dates.

Brainstormed Ideas

	SUGGESTED BY	PRIORITY (A, B, C)
Variance in times report should be generated	Jamie A.	B
Lack of communication between departments regarding changes	Bill J.	A
Shipping procedures not being followed properly by Sales personnel	Nancy B.	A
Reports not being read properly	Bob M.	C
Delivery Service personnel not recording ship date accurately	Jamie A.	B
Customer Service personnel not checking schedule revisions list regularly	Carl U.	A
Delivery service computers not accurate	Steve M.	C
Weekend data entry throwing off the system	Bob M.	A
Invoices getting lost—poeple making up dates	Jamie A.	B

Brainstorming Guidelines

1. Select a facilitator.
2. Establish a time limit (4-7 minutes).
3. Stimulate team participation (no critical feedback).
4. Prioritize ideas (A, B, C).

BRAINSTORMING

The Brainstorming form allows team members to have a record of their efforts when brainstorming. Often, the causes to a problem or possible ideas for a solution that are brainstormed are forgotten because they were not recorded.

To complete this form, follow the sequence listed below:

1. Describe the reason for brainstorming in the "Situation" section.
2. Have the meeting recorder list the ideas offered as they are presented beneath the column heading "Brainstormed Ideas."
3. Identify the individual who offered his or her idea and record his or her name or initials under the "Suggested By" column.
4. After ideas have been exhausted, have the team determine priorities of each idea and rank them (e.g., A, B, C). Priority A items should be addressed first or viewed as more critical to the situation needs and objectives.

TIP #1: Select a facilitator to guide the group through the brainstorming exercise. It is often wise to have someone from outside the group serve as facilitator.

TIP #2: Introduce either the round-robin or free-for-all methods of brainstorming. The *round-robin* method of brainstorming requires that you begin with one individual and proceed to each successive member around the room. The *free-for-all* is commonly used and allows the group to offer their ideas spontaneously without waiting for their turn as would be common to the round-robin method.

TIP #3: Establish a short time period for brainstorming to take place. Recommended time would be four to seven minutes. A short time span ignites creative thinking.

TIP #4: During the brainstorming session, do not allow team members to criticize or comment on ideas. Wait for all ideas to be exhausted before returning to defining and/or prioritizing each idea.

TIP #5: After it appears that the group has exhausted the ideas, have the group prioritize each idea as an A, B, or C.

- Priority A items represent ideas the group believes will have the greatest impact, or offer the greatest assistance.
- Priority B items are important but will need to wait until all priority A items have been addressed.
- Priority C items represent ideas or suggestions the group believes offer the least amount of assistance and should not be addressed until all priority A and B items have been pursued.

TIP #6: Provide copies of the Brainstorming form to all group members.

TIP #7: Keep a copy of the completed Brainstorming form in either the team file or the file associated with the problem at hand.

Check Sheet FORM 9

The Check Sheet form should be used whenever an individual or team needs to collect data in order to determine trends. This tool answers the simple question, "How often are specified events happening?"

Check Sheet

Focus

Delays due to computer problems.

Category	FREQUENCY	TOTALS
Registration program not archiving properly.	I I I I	4
Unable to fax through computer.	I I	2
Too many network shutdowns.	I	1
Computer locks up when running more than one application.	I I I	3
	FINAL TOTAL	10

Where Data Was Collected: Data Entry
When Data Was Collected: November 6-20
Data Collected By: Duane Chandler

CHECK SHEET

The Check Sheet form provides a numerical format in which to separate the opinions voiced by people from actual facts. Collected data represents the frequency of identified occurrences that take place within a specified period of time. Such data is helpful in problem-solving situations where root causes are trying to be determined.

To complete this form, follow the sequence listed below:

1. Identify the focus.
2. In the "Category" column, record the nature of the occurrence that will be observed and tracked.
3. As each specific occurrence is observed, record a single hash mark in the "Frequency" column. On the fifth occurrence, draw the fifth hash mark through the four standing marks. This allows you to separate the total occurrences for any one category item into groups of five.
4. At the conclusion of the time period, add each category item separately and record the total in the "Total" column.
5. Record where data was collected.
6. Record when data was collected.
7. Record who collected the data.

TIP #1: If more than one person is collecting data, be sure that everyone has a Check Sheet with the correct category items listed.

TIP #2: Consider shorter times for collecting data if the frequency is expected to be great. Data collection can be extended if frequency of occurrences is expected to be small.

TIP #3: Remember, *frequency* represents only how often something is occurring! It does not define why something is occurring.

TIP #4: Collected data can assist you in prioritizing causes by frequency totals. However, it is wise to also assess the labor or financial costs associated with specific occurrences.

TIP #5: The frequency totals are often used to create Pareto Charts. (A *Pareto Chart* is a special type of bar graph that helps identify which problems should be solved based on the impact made by the problem.)

TIP #6: The completed Check Sheet should be kept on file for future reference and statistical justification.

Process Interruption Analysis FORM 10

This form is used to identify how much time is wasted because of delays and interruptions to the normal work flow process.

Process Interruption Analysis

EMPLOYEE Bill Smith

DEPARTMENT Commercial Accounts

TOTAL TIME 9 hours, 8 minutes

OF DAYS COLLECTED 10

DATE	INTERRUPTION	TIME								HOURS
1/8	Re-explain account	From	10:30	2:00						Regular
	information to	To	10:50	2:15						Overtime
	various departments.	Minutes	20	15					35	Total
1/9	Phone system out	From	9:00							Regular
	due to storm.	To	9:30							Overtime
		Minutes	30						30	Total
1/9	Power outage in office.	From	12:00	3:00						Regular
		To	12:15	3:15						Overtime
		Minutes	15	15					30	Total
1/10	Reinstall software	From	11:00							Regular
	on laptop.	To	11:45							Overtime
		Minutes	45						45	Total
1/11	Attend meeting for	From	8:00							Regular
	another account.	To	8:30							Overtime
		Minutes	30						30	Total
1/12	Surprise visit by	From	7:30							Regular
	major supplier.	To	9:00							Overtime
		Minutes	90						90	Total
1/15	Paperwork delay—	From	11:30							Regular
	waiting for report.	To	11:45							Overtime
		Minutes	15						15	Total
1/16	Printer problems.	From	1:00	4:15						Regular
		To	1:20	4:30						Overtime
		Minutes	20	15					35	Total
1/17	Clarify client	From	1:00							Regular
	information with	To	2:00							Overtime
	Accounting dept.	Minutes	60						60	Total

PROCESS INTERRUPTION ANALYSIS

The Process Interruption Analysis form allows an individual, department, or team to record the nature of interruptions experienced during a workday and the time spent dealing with the interruption. This form can be used to spot potential time wasters created by internal sources; assess the efficiency of equipment, computers, and so on; or identify if present customer service is adequate.

To complete this form, follow the sequence listed below:

1. Record the name of the individual who will be collecting data and his or her department name.
2. After data collection is completed, record the total time of interruptions that were experienced and the number of days data was collected.
3. As interruptions occur, record the correct date, nature of interruption, and the time in which the interruption occurred (e.g., 10:00–10:15).
4. Record the total minutes for each interruption.
5. Record totals for interrupted time in the "Time" section, making sure that time is recorded next to appropriate "Hours" section.

TIP #1: If the nature of interruptions is known, record those interruptions ahead of time. This will allow you to then record any time wasted for only those selected items.

TIP #2: Be as accurate as possible with times. Therefore, keep a watch or clock close to work area.

TIP #3: If the time wasted is directly accounted to overtime, then that time should be recorded accordingly in the "Hour" section by placing an "O" by the time.

TIP #4: Notice the trend of interruptions. You may observe that some interruptions happen with less frequency, but cause a greater amount of down time. (This is why the Check Sheet alone does not always provide the most accurate picture of loss time.)

TIP #5: When an interruption is repeated, be sensitive to the time involvement for each occurrence.

TIP #6: The total time results can be used to create a Pareto Chart. (See comments about Pareto Charts on Check Sheet form description.)

Cause and Effect Chart FORM 11

This form reflects the relationship between a specific problem, or effect, and the causes that impact the effect.

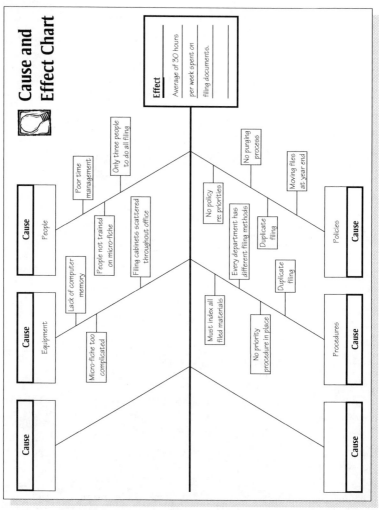

CAUSE AND EFFECT CHART

The Cause and Effect Chart form provides a method to observe all possible causes contributing to some observable effect. The causes are placed into categories that provide clarity and distinction. This effort will help you to see areas of causes that may have more or less impact on the effect. This form is usually used as part of a team problem-solving effort.

To complete this form, follow the sequence listed below:

1. First, record the observable problem in the "Effect" box on the right side of the chart.
2. Identify the cause categories and record those that are appropriate to your situation. For example, in manufacturing environments, common cause categories often include the six M's: money, machines, management, method, manpower, and materials.
3. If the six M's are not appropriate, consider using category names more applicable to your workplace, for example, policies, personnel, procedures, or process.
4. Use the Brainstorming form (#8), to brainstorm possible causes to an effect. Take the brainstorming results and place each brainstormed idea onto the Cause and Effect Chart in the most appropriate category(ies).
5. Draw a short line off of the main category "vein" to record the specific brainstormed item. Record other ideas in similar manner. As more ideas are recorded, the chart begins to take on a skeleton like appearance of a fish. This chart is also recognized as the Fishbone Diagram.

TIP #1: Some brainstormed ideas may fit appropriately in more than one cause category.

TIP #2: Look at each of the four to six cause categories to identify the number of items recorded. A cause category that has many items may be an indication of the root cause leading to the effect.

TIP #3: Look for individual causes that are recorded in more than one category. Occasionally, causes that are showing up in several categories may indicate a root cause that should be assessed more closely.

TIP #4: Once the Cause and Effect Chart has been completed, the team can then discern what cause may have a greater impact on the effect.

TIP #5: If one clear cause is not evident, have the team identify the top three to four possible causes and collect data to assess the impact made by each cause.

Stairstepping (Five Whys)   FORM 12

This form assists in identifying a root cause to a problem by asking "Why" five times.

Stairstepping (Five Whys)

Problem

Catalogs with errors in them are being mailed to customers.

Why #1

Why are catalogs with errors in them being mailed to customers?

Insufficient proofreading.

Why #2

Why is there insufficient proofreading?

Proofreaders didn't know some of the information was wrong.

Why #3

Why didn't proofreaders know some information was wrong?

Various departments didn't send a master list of correct data.

Why #4

Why didn't each department send a master list of data?

Lack of communication and directions.

Why #5

Why is there a lack of communication and direction?

No single project manager overseeing the project.

STAIRSTEPPING

The Stairstepping form is to be used only after a brainstorming session has occurred. The form allows a team to identify the deeper root of a problem. If applied correctly, a solution to a problem may be only a few questions away.

To complete this form, follow the sequence listed below:

1. First record the problem statement, or nature of the effect, that the team is trying to resolve.
2. Ask "Why" the stated problem is a problem. Record the response right below the question.
3. Then address the first response by asking "Why" and record the team's response below that question. Follow this same procedure until the "Why" question has been asked for each successive level. Each response should be more narrow in focus.
4. When the final "Why" is asked, allow the team to assess the root response at the top of the chart.

TIP #1: Asking "Why" five times will be uncomfortable initially. Keep asking the question "Why" and only accept a response that narrows the focus of the problem.

TIP #2: If your team has already created a Cause and Effect Chart, you may want to answer your first "Why" with a cause item from the Cause and Effect Chart. Then proceed to narrow the focus for this particular cause.

TIP #3: You may conduct the stairstepping process on several causes. You will find that the time spent here can expedite the process of finding a solution.

TIP #4: If more than one response is possible for any "Why" response, record the multiple responses near the question and number each response. You'll then need to ask "Why" for each numbered item and separate the responses, by number, for the next level up.

Problem Analysis FORM 13

 When the root cause to a problem needs identification, the Problem Analysis form helps to separate what is occurring from what one would expect to occur, but is not occurring.

Sample Problem

Like many other corporations, ACME Inc. had just completed a large reorganization process. Early retirements, transfers, and departmental shifts were all part of the move to bring more people to the corporate headquarters in Kansas City.

ACME was operating out of a number of buildings clustered together while plans were being made to construct a giant facility that would bring everyone together under one roof. In the meantime, the reorganization meant a lot of shuffling around of people from one building to another, or from one office to another within the same building. As far as anyone could tell, the moves went smoothly with a minimum of resistance.

Unfortunately, a couple of months later, things were different. Complaints began coming in from many administrative assistants. At first they voiced dissatisfaction with things. Dissatisfaction gave way to unhappiness and eventually, outright anger. The disgruntled administrative assistants complained that nothing worked: the new computers they had been given didn't work properly, their desks weren't level, the air conditioning was too loud, and management decisions were getting poor reviews. All attempts at retrieving hard data in order to solve these problems were met with resistance and interpreted by the assistants as a lack of trust.

A noticeable drop in productivity resulted and a few administrative assistants left the company. Before things got worse and more key people quit, a thorough examination of the situation was made using the Problem Analysis form.

Problem Analysis

Problem Statement

Administrative assistants complaints increasing, 3 resignations, and a decrease in productivity.

Problem Characteristic	Is (Actual)	Is Not (Would Expect, But Not)	Need Information
What/Who:			
OBJECT/PROCESS PERSON	Administrative assistants	Other people in their departments	What is the nature of their complaints? Are all assistants complaining?
DEFECT/PROBLEM	Unusual number of complaints and resignations	Complaints about salary or lack of training	Have assistants had a history of complaining?
Where:			
SEEN ON OBJECT/ IN WORKFORCE	Three departments: Accounting, Purchasing, & Research & Development	One centralized department	What is unique to those three departments?
SEEN WITHIN PROCESS	At the administrative assistant level	All levels of employees	What is unique to admin. assistants in those three departments?
When:			
INITIALLY SEEN	After July 4 holiday	Any other time	What happened before July 4 holiday? After?
OTHER TIMES OBSERVED	Throughout month of July	Previous months	Has there ever been a history of particular assistants complaining?
How:			
MANY OBJECTS/ PERSONS HAVE DEFECTS/ PROBLEMS?	Received "official" complaints from 20 assistants	And who match criteria of new computers, same building, & some managers	Are the complaints about the same things or a variety of issues?
MANY DEFECTS/ PROBLEMS PER OBJECT/PERSON?	N/A	N/A	
AFFECTING OTHER OBJECTS/AREAS PEOPLE?	At present, none / At present, none	Other mid-level employees such as support staff	Is there agreement from other employees about nature of complaints?

PROBLEM ANALYSIS

The Problem Analysis form addresses the what or who, where, when, and how questions about a problem. Following a sequence of questions will help you to identify a variance. A *variance* is the difference between what is expected from what is actually being experienced. Often, a variance will point you to the correct root cause, making the problem-solving effort more effective and efficient.

To complete this form, follow the sequence listed below:

1. Describe the problem in the "Problem Statement" section.
2. Identify what object, process, or person is experiencing the problem. Record your answer under the "Is" column for the "Object/Process/Person" row.
3. Identify what object, process, or person would also be expected to experience the problem but is not. Record your answer under the "Is Not" column for the "Object/Process/Person" row.
4. If your first two written responses are different, what information would be helpful to understand the difference? Record your question in the "Need Information" section for the "Object/Process/Person" row.
5. What is the actual defect or problem? Record your answer under the "Is" column for the "Defect/Problem" row.
6. What defect or problem would you expect to occur but is not? Record your answer under the "Is Not" column for the "Defect/Problem" row.
7. If your two written responses are different, what information would be helpful to understand the difference? Record your question in the "Need Information" column for the "Defect/Problem" row.
8. The same method of asking questions should be applied for the where, when, and how of the "Problem Characteristic" column. Always move one column and row at a time, recording your responses in the appropriate row.

9. After you have responded to the "Is" and "Is Not" for each row, be sure to record any questions you might have that require more information in the "Need Information" section.

TIP #1: Proceed through the Problem Analysis form one problem characteristic at a time.

TIP #2: Be sensitive to the difference between the "Is" and "Is Not" column responses. Remember, any difference may lead you to the root cause of a problem.

TIP #3: For each difference observed, record what information you would like to have that might explain the difference in responses in the "Is" and "Is Not" column.

TIP #4: The Problem Analysis form should be used when you are having difficulty identifying a root cause to a problem.

TIP #5: If any question on the Problem Analysis form is not applicable for the problem being addressed, simply record "N/A" (Not Applicable) in the appropriate section.

TIP #6: Consider the following definitions for the problem characteristic questions:

• *What* refers to what the object or process is that is experiencing the problem.
• *Who* refers to any person or group of people who is experiencing the problem.
• *Where* refers to where on the object, in the process, or in the workforce the problem is being experienced.
• *When* refers to when the problem is observed on the object, in the process, or among the workforce.
• *How* refers to the quantity of occurrences that is being experienced.

Negotiables and Non-Negotiables

FORM 14

When developing a solution, identify the boundaries to stay within to be acceptable and successful. The Negotiables and Non-Negotiables form can identify any criteria that cannot be changed (non-negotiable) and any criteria that can be modified (negotiable).

Negotiables and Non-Negotiables

End-Result Description

Increased staffing in Customer Service Department

Non-Negotiables	Negotiables
Word processing and spreadsheet experience	Can be a new hire or transfer from other department
Cross-trained to handle different tasks	Previous sales experience preferred, but not required
Post High-School degree	Telephone skills
Minimum two years experience in specified field	Technical degree or college degree

Potential Solutions

1. Shift personnel around within organization.
2. Begin flex-time schedule to stagger hours of people in department.

NEGOTIABLES AND NON-NEGOTIABLES

The Negotiables and Non-Negotiables form provides you with the chance to understand the criteria that must be in place before a solution is implemented. The benefit of this form is that it can keep a team from working hard to develop a solution only to have it rejected from upper management because the solution did not meet certain criteria.

To complete this form, follow the sequence listed below:

1. Record an end-result description that describes the ideal result. This description should reflect the positive activities, improvements, results, and so on that can be expected with a correct solution.

2. Consider any condition, requirement, policy, rule, restriction, and so on that cannot be changed. Record such items in the "Non-Negotiables" column.

3. Record any criteria that offers some flexibility in the "Negotiables" column. For example, a non-negotiable for purchasing new computers might be a budget restriction of $25,000. The negotiable might be that any brand of computer can be bought.

4. Once the negotiables and non-negotiables have been recorded, list any potential solutions that appear to fit within the boundaries established.

TIP #1: When brainstorming for non-negotiables, consider obvious criteria such as dates, budget restrictions, needed sign-off from senior management, and company policies or procedures.

TIP #2: For each non-negotiable, consider the possible areas surrounding the strict boundary requirement that is negotiable and record such items.

TIP #3: If you arrive at a solution before developing the negotiables and non-negotiables, complete the form before making any presentation. It could save you time and embarrassment.

FLO-PERT Chart FORM 15

When changing an old process to a new process, you will need to make the appropriate plans. The FLO-PERT Chart allows you to identify the what, who, and when involved with the new process steps.

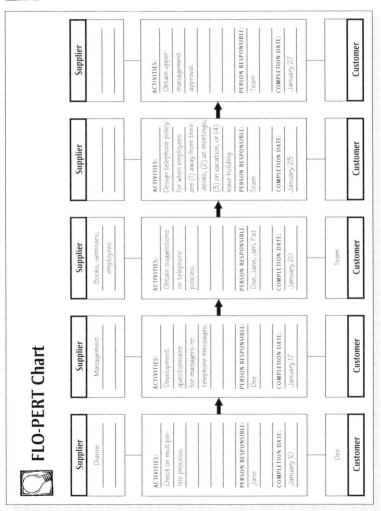

FLO-PERT Chart

Supplier
Dianne

ACTIVITIES:
Check on multiple-line process.

PERSON RESPONSIBLE:
Jane

COMPLETION DATE:
January 10

Customer
Dee

Supplier
Management

ACTIVITIES:
Development questionnaire for managers re: telephone messages.

PERSON RESPONSIBLE:
Dee

COMPLETION DATE:
January 17

Customer

Supplier
Books, seminars, employees

ACTIVITIES:
Obtain suggestions on telephone policies.

PERSON RESPONSIBLE:
Dee, Jane, Jen, Pat

COMPLETION DATE:
January 20

Customer
Team

Supplier

ACTIVITIES:
Design telephone policy for when employees are (1) away from their desks, (2) at meetings, (3) on vacation, or (4) leave building.

PERSON RESPONSIBLE:
Team

COMPLETION DATE:
January 23

Customer

Supplier

ACTIVITIES:
Obtain upper-management approval.

PERSON RESPONSIBLE:
Team

COMPLETION DATE:
January 27

Customer

FLO-PERT CHART

The FLO-PERT Chart combines the strengths of two processes: the flow chart and the Performance Evaluation and Review Technique (PERT) Chart. Flow charts allow you to write down the sequence of steps in any process. PERT Charts provide the who, what, and when information for each step, allowing you to review the performance of each step. Together, the FLO-PERT Chart combines the convenience of showing the flow of a process and the measurable components of each step.

To complete this form, follow the sequence listed below:

1. Starting with an agreed upon solution, list the steps to implement the solution.
2. After listing the steps, prioritize the steps beginning with step one, two, three, and so on.
3. Record the first step in the first box next to the "Activities" section.
4. Identify the person who will be responsible for a specific activity in the "Person Responsible" section.
5. Next, record the completion date for the activity in the "Completion Date" section.
6. For each activity, consider any person, department, or company that might provide a resource to the person completing the activity. Record the name of any person, department, or company in the "Supplier" section.
7. Record the name of the person who will be effected by the activity in the "Customer" section.
8. Repeat steps 3 to 7 for each solution step identified.

TIP #1: If there are activities that must be completed at the same time, you may record them in the same section or record them separately.

TIP #2: If you do record more than one activity within the same section, number or color code each activity step to maintain order and clarity.

TIP #3: The name identified under "Person Responsible" does not necessarily have to be the individual actually completing the activity. He or she is, however, responsible for ensuring the activity's completion.

TIP #4: It's often wise to include telephone numbers for any customers or suppliers identified.

TIP #5: Each person involved or impacted with this change in process should receive a copy of the FLO-PERT Chart.

TIP #6: Traditionally, a PERT Chart is completed by working backward. Starting with an end result in mind, a team would list the last step to be completed, then repeat this process until they arrived at the beginning step. This is difficult to do at first, but the backward planning does tend to keep a team from overlooking any step and also demands that the team consider the amount of time any step may need.

TIP #7: If you use the backward technique, use a marker board to list your steps. This will allow you to make corrections easier before committing the final progression of steps to the FLO-PERT Chart.

Action Plan FORM 16

When a solution to a problem has been developed, the Action Plan form can be used to create the implementation schedule for the solution.

Action Plan

DEPARTMENT Human Resources   SPONSOR Gary Holle

Goal

Train each employee on new computer system within next 90 days (TEAM: Techies).

ACTION STEPS	PEOPLE RESPONSIBLE	COMPLETION DATE	RESOURCES NEEDED
1. Coordinate with software company for a trainer and training schedule.	Susan	June 1	
2. Divide employees into groups of ten for classes.	Joe, Mary	June 6	Department rosters
3. Reserve computer training rooms at local college.	Gary	June 9	
4. Publish training schedule and coordinate conflicts with department manager.	Jeff, Linda	June 12	Travel schedules
5. Pick up manuals and distribute.	Susan	June 15	
6. Begin class.	All	June 20	

ACTION PLAN

When your team or department solves a problem, the solution may require several steps for implementation. The Action Plan form represents the documented steps of a solution that, when completed, will correct a problem. The form identifies what will be done, who will take the action, when the action will be completed, and what resources will be needed to implement each step.

To complete this form, follow the sequence listed below:

1. Identify what department or team is involved with the action plan.
2. Identify a sponsor for the action plan. The sponsor will be the contact person for the plan. (The sponsor could be a manager within your organization or one of the individuals from the problem-solving team.)
3. Record each action step in the order that the steps will be executed.
4. Identify the people responsible for each step and record their name.
5. Record the completion date for each step.
6. Any source of information that will be needed for each step to be completed should be recorded in the "Resources Needed" section. (Resources could include information, telephone numbers, money, equipment, charts, or statistics.)

TIP #1: Be sure that the sponsor is someone who will keep your team accountable to implementing the solution.

TIP #2: Have your team brainstorm all of the needed steps before putting them into sequential order.

TIP #3: If several steps have the same completion date, record the time each step will be completed.

TIP #4: Don't overlook any resource an individual step may need. Often, when a solution is being implemented, resources as simple as telephone numbers, purchase order numbers, or appropriate identification can disrupt the solution process.

TIP #5: Everyone that is part of the solution process should have a copy of the Action Plan.

TIP #6: If any changes occur, simply make the necessary modifications and forward an amended Action Plan to all parties involved.

TIP #7: If the plan will take place over a lengthy period of time, schedule Action Plan updates. A formal update meeting should be scheduled and made part of the Action Plan.

Customer/Supplier-Relationship Tools

Customer/Supplier Requirements FORM 17

All work processes run more efficiently when clearly defined needs and requirements of customers and suppliers are communicated.

Customer/Supplier Requirements

☑ Customer
☐ Supplier

DEPARTMENT: Publications   DATE: February 16

CONTACT: Mike Bradley   PHONE: x245

Needs & Requirements	How Measured
Articles should be submitted one month in advance of publication.	Posted calendar on department wall.
Articles must follow formatting policy.	Check against department formats and styles.
Advertisers should proof their own material.	Number of mistakes caught.
Rewrites due 3 days after issued.	Posted calendar on department wall.

Obstacles/Barriers	How to Resolve
Not everyone's computer is set up with correct word-processing formats and styles.	Data Processing Department to set up all computers with acceptable styles.
Can't get rewrites to out-of-town individuals.	Purchase fax software for all field personnel.

Gene Harmon
COLLECTED BY

GH
CUSTOMER/SUPPLIER INITIALS

Customer/Supplier-Relationship Tools

CUSTOMER/SUPPLIER REQUIREMENTS

The Customer/Supplier Requirements form is a communication tool for all customer and supplier relationships, both internal and external. It asks both parties to give specific instructions on what they need from the other in order to be successful, and the form also provides a system by which the level of success can be measured.

To complete this form, follow the sequence listed below:

1. First identify if the form is being filled out by a customer or supplier by checking the appropriate box at the top.
2. Fill out the details regarding the team or department, the date, who the contact person is for the customer/supplier, and the telephone number where he or she can be reached.
3. List specific needs and requirements you have for either your customer or supplier.
4. In the "How Measured" section, provide information on how your team or department will measure your customer's or supplier's success in meeting your needs and requirements.
5. List all potential obstacles/barriers that may be experienced, either by your team or your customer/supplier, that will have to be overcome in order to fulfill the requirements.
6. Offer a brief list of possible solutions to the previously mentioned obstacles in the "How to Resolve" section.
7. Finally, make sure someone from the team who prepares the form signs it and gets a signature from the customer/supplier.

TIP #1: Be as specific as possible when listing needs and requirements. The more specific the requirement, the easier it will be to measure its success.

TIP #2: Be realistic. List only needs and requirements.

TIP #3: As a team, don't go back only to your suppliers with this form, also give it to your customers for their input.

TIP #4: Schedule a meeting with your customer/supplier to discuss the level of success in meeting needs and requirements.

Customer Needs Analysis FORM 18

This form is directed solely to your team's or department's customer and it is a questionnaire asking your customer to respond to your service or product quality.

Customer Needs Analysis

CUSTOMER Midwest Organizations   DATE January 29

1. What product/service do we provide you?
Computers and accessories

2. Does your product/service meet your needs? Why?
Yes. You advised me on the proper specifications for my computers, which will meet my needs for the next several years.

3. What improvements can we make regarding our product/service quality?
Sometimes I'm on "hold" too long when I call.

4. What service do you need us to provide you regarding how we:
a. Bring our product to you? Call before delivery so we can clear furniture and be prepared.

b. Follow-up? Next day phone call would be great.

c. Communicate? Let us know as soon as possible if a delivery is to be delayed.

d. Alert you to changes? Not necessary, your monthly flyers are great.

5. When do you prefer to have product/services provided?
Any time but the noon hour.

6. How do you prefer delivery of our product/service?
No special preferences.

CUSTOMER NEEDS ANALYSIS

Maintaining close contact with your customers is just good business. Whether the customers are internal or external, your job is to keep them happy. This form can be used on a regular basis to keep the lines of communication open with your customers by getting their feedback on your performance.

To complete this form, follow the sequence listed below:

1. Identify the customer who will fill out the Customer Needs Analysis form.
2. Include with the form a letter explaining who is sending the form and what you hope to gain from it.
3. Deliver it to your customer in the most appropriate manner.

TIP #1: Ask your customer to be as honest and specific as possible.

TIP #2: Respond to your customer immediately after receiving the form. Delays in response time will send a bad signal to your customer.

TIP #3: Keep a record of each analysis to discuss in meetings. Some forms may serve as a stimulus for a problem-solving effort.

Customer/Supplier Performance Index

FORM 19

Providing feedback to customers and suppliers is critical if you want to build healthy work relationships. This form is a "scorecard" that tracks the performance of a customer or supplier over a seven-day period.

Customer/Supplier Performance Index

☐ Customer
☑ Supplier

NAME Sales Department   DATE February 9

Needs/Requirements	DAY 1	DAY 2	DAY 3	DAY 4	DAY 5	DAY 6	DAY 7
Reports due by noon on Friday	MPN	MPN	BPN*	MPN	MPN	MPN	MPN
Provides customer change update list	MPN	EPN#	MPN	MPN	MPN	MPN	MPN
New customer list due at end of business day	EPN**	MPN	MPN	MPN	BPN##	MPN	MPN
Call five new potential clients daily	MPN	MPN	MPN	MPN	BPN***	MPN	MPN

Grades

BPN = BELOW PERFORMANCE NEEDS
MPN = MEETS PERFORMANCE NEEDS
EPN = EXCEEDS PERFORMANCE NEEDS

Daily Comments

* Received report at end of day on Friday.

\# Already entered customer changes in system.

** Report delivered 1 hour ahead of schedule.

\#\# Received one day late.

*** Received reports of two new calls.

CUSTOMER/SUPPLIER PERFORMANCE INDEX

The Customer/Supplier Requirements and Customer Needs Analysis forms help to establish standards of performance in the customer/supplier relationship. The Customer/Supplier Performance Index form takes those standards (needs and requirements) and provides a rating scale so a scorecard can be developed. The form also includes a section for comments to explain special circumstances on a particular day.

To complete this form, follow the sequence listed below:

1. Identify the customer or supplier you will be sending the form to, and check the appropriate box at the top of the form.
2. Using the Customer/Supplier Requirements form, list the needs/requirements in the appropriate column.
3. For each need/requirement, grade the fulfillment of that requirement using the following grades:

   a. BPN = Below Performance Needs
   b. MPN = Meets Performance Needs
   c. EPN = Exceeds Performance Needs

4. If there are special circumstances surrounding an event on a particular day, write those in the "Daily Comments" section for the corresponding day.

TIP #1: Make sure the needs and requirements are specific enough to measure.

TIP #2: Be consistent in your grading. You are looking for trends and/or repeat problems that need to be addressed.

TIP #3: Share the scorecard with the customer/supplier you are grading. Be sure to give them accurate feedback.

TIP #4: Sometimes a supplier can exceed performance needs, and it cause problems. Be sure to address such issues because many times suppliers think they may doing your group a favor.

OFI Alert FORM 20

The Opportunity for Improvement (OFI) form illustrates the negative impact an error committed by the supplier has on the customer.

OFI Alert

NAME Susan Williams   PHONE ×267

TITLE Data Entry   DATE April 15

Identify the Originating Department or Supplier

Tom Helm —Adjuster

Describe the Supplier's Opportunity for Improvement (OFI)

Filling out claim forms correctly will increase total productivity and decrease response time to policyholder. The problem is not wrong calculations but improper use of form. This slows down the process because once I catch mistakes, I have to send the paperwork back, have you fill it out again, and then I have to reenter it into the computer.

Quantify Your Lost Productivity Due to the OFI

Labor Expense

COST/HOUR	X	# OF PEOPLE	X	HOURS/PERSON	=	TOTAL LABOR COST
$ 10.00		1		4		$ 40.00

Equipment Expense

COST/MACHINE	X	# OF MACHINES	X	HOURS/MACHINE	=	TOTAL EQUIPMENT COST
$ 5.00		1		4		$ 20.00

Material Expense

COST/UNIT	X	# OF UNITS			=	TOTAL MATERIAL COST
$ 20.00		2				$ 40.00

Total Cost due to Non-Conformance $ 100.00

Supplier Evaluation & Follow-Up

HAVE ACTIONS BEEN TAKEN TO PREVENT RECURRENCE?   ☑ YES   ☐ NO   ☐ IN PROCESS

IF YES, LIST ACTIONS BEING TAKEN AND WHEN THEY WILL TAKE EFFECT:
Tom did not receive proper training on report procedures. He will be trained and watched next week.

HOW DO YOU PLAN TO MONITOR THE SUCCESS OF YOUR CORRECTIVE ACTIONS?
Tom will be responsible for checking each claim prior to sending it to data entry.

RESPONDENT'S NAME Tom Helm   DATE April 17

Copy and return this form to customer upon completion

OFI ALERT

Used as a compliment to the Customer/Supplier Performance Index form, the OFI Alert form highlights a need or requirement that is constantly performed below performance needs and is decreasing a team's, department's, or individual's productivity and efficiency. These decreases can be quantified and explained on the form. The OFI Alert is also a good feedback form because its completion requires the "offending" party to detail what it has done to eliminate the problem.

To complete this form, follow the sequence listed below:

1. Fill in pertinent information: name, title, telephone number, and date.
2. Use the "Identify the Originating Department or Supplier" section to specify the individual or group that has passed along a deficient product or service.
3. Detail the problem and what the improvement will do for your productivity and efficiency in the "Describe the Supplier's Opportunity for Improvement" section.
4. Calculate the financial impact the supplier's OFI is having on you in terms of time, equipment cost, and material expense in the "Quantify Your Lost Productivity Due to OFI" section.
5. Return the OFI Alert form to the supplier and have the supplier fill out the "Supplier Evaluation and Follow-up" section.
6. Have the supplier return the form to you and keep it on file as documentation that the problem has been solved.

TIP #1: Keep the process of filling out this form positive. Approach the erring supplier with a constructive attitude, not a blaming one. Remember, there may be constraints on the supplier that are causing the error.

TIP #2: Be realistic with the financial section of the form. Exaggerating numbers will only complicate the process.

TIP #3: When giving the form back to the supplier, give him or her a target date for completing and returning the form.

TIP #4: Keep all OFI Alert forms filed with other important team documents for future reference.

Project-Assessment
Forms

Project Overview FORM 21

Whenever a problem-solving or improvement effort requires a formal presentation, the Project Overview form provides a one page overview of what is currently being experienced and recommendations for the proposed solution.

Project Overview

NAME PC Players   DATE March 6

Project Description

Our cross-departmental team was formed to analyze the increasing workload on administrative assistants. After months of interviews and data collection, it was determined that most of the increased workload includes writing letters and memos, simple filing, and generating reports. Because most of the employees do not have computers, everyone is dependent on a few individuals (administrative assistants) to do more than they are capable of handling.

Present Method

We are currently using a four-year-old mainframe computer to do the bulk of the computer work in the office. Therefore, a "typing pool" of administrative assistants was created. Data collected revealed that the administrative assistants, after creating their own schedule to work in the typing pool, are getting behind in their other duties, on average two hours a week.

Proposed Method

New personal computers should be purchased for all office personnel, thus freeing up the mainframe computer. The results of a survey issued reveal that 93% of all employees are literate in personal computing skills, meaning a minimum of training would be required to reach "up-to-speed" results.

Expected Benefits

A 25% improvement in productivity of all employees, which would reduce waiting time for documents to be typed. A 25% improvement in accuracy of administrative assistants "regular" duties. A 20% reduction in paper costs. A 25% increase in speed of service to internal customers and suppliers that need information.

Required to Implement

$90,000 for computers ($1,800 x 50)
$3,000 for printers
$10,000 consultant fees for converting data from mainframe computer
$1,000 in furniture for computers and printers

PROJECT OVERVIEW

Whenever a solution or improvement effort requires capital moneys, a justification for such moneys is often required. The Project Overview is a one page summary of what an individual or team proposes, as well as expected benefits and financial needs for the proposal. Attach other needed documentation to this form to provide greater details.

To complete this form, follow the sequence listed below:

1. Record the name of the person, department, or team that is submitting the overview and the date it is submitted.
2. The "Project Description" section should include the primary purpose of the project and what information the team has developed about the problem or the improvement needed.
3. Define the present method regarding the current situation.
4. The team's proposed method should be recorded in the appropriate section.
5. List the expected benefits in the appropriate section. It is especially important to list projected performance improvements that tie directly to the proposed method.
6. The needed moneys, time, labor, and so on should be listed in the "Required to Implement" section.

TIP #1: The Project Overview form serves as a cover-sheet summary for the documents attached.

TIP #2: There should be less detail involved with the "Present Method" and "Proposed Method" sections because the attached documentation will provide that needed information.

TIP #3: Any performance improvements expected should be conservative and expressed as a percentage improvement.

TIP #4: There should be appropriate financial information to support each dollar amount being requested in the "Required to Implement" section.

TIP #5: If you are making a formal presentation, make copies of the form for each member of the audience.

Proposed Investment Expense (PIE)

FORM 22

This form reflects the anticipated expenses to implement a proposed solution.

Proposed Investment Expense (PIE)

NAME _PC Players_   DATE _March 6_

Project Description

Purchase PCs for every office employee and printers for each department.

Labor Expense

COST/HOUR	X	# OF PEOPLE	X	# HOURS/DAY	=	TOTAL LABOR COST/DAY
$ 15.00		10		8		$ 1,200.00

INCLUDES
Setting up PCs on everyone's desk, installing printers in department work rooms, and removing mainframe.

Equipment Expense

COST	X	# OF MACHINES		=	TOTAL EQUIPMENT COST
$ 1,800.00		50			$ 90,000.00

INCLUDES
Cost of computers with monitor and software, 5 printers, and 20 computer stands.

Material Expense

UNIT COST	X	# OF UNITS		=	TOTAL UNIT COST
$ 20.00		25			$ 500.00

INCLUDES
Surge protectors, cords, cables, etc.

Total Investment $ 91,700.00

PROPOSED INVESTMENT EXPENSE

The Proposed Investment Expense form identifies the investment costs that your organization will experience for a proposed solution. The costs could be for purchasing equipment, adding staff, or updating computers.

To complete this form, follow the sequence listed below:

1. Record the name of the person, department, or team that is submitting the proposal and the date of submittal.

2. In the "Project Description" section, describe the actual proposed request.

3. In the "Labor Expense" section, record the expected costs associated with any labor investment. There are five components for this section.

   a. The "Cost/Hour" represents the average hourly rate of the employees involved with the solution.

   b. The "# of People" is the total number of individuals involved with the solution.

   c. The "# Hours/Day" reflects the total time expected to be invested per day by the individuals involved.

   d. The "Total Labor Cost/Day" is the total labor expense per day to implement the solution.

   e. A brief description explaining how the "Labor Expense" dollars will be spent should be documented in the "Includes" section.

4. The "Equipment Expense" section projects expected costs associated with purchasing new equipment or for updating existing equipment. There are four components to this section.

   a. The "Cost" represents the actual unit cost for each piece of new equipment to be purchased or the individual updating cost for each piece of existing equipment.

   b. The "# of Machines" is the total number of machines to be purchased or updated.

c. The "Total Equipment Cost" reflects the total costs to purchase or update all the proposed equipment.

d. Details of the "Total Equipment Costs" can be recorded in the "Includes" section.

5. The "Material Expense" section projects any other material purchases that will be made. Often, this area reflects items that may directly support the equipment to be purchased or the people who will be operating the new equipment. There are four components to this section.

a. "Unit Cost" represents the total cost associated with items needed to support one piece of equipment.

b. "# of Units" represents the number of support items that will be needed to adequately support all equipment purchases.

c. The "Total Unit Cost" reflects the total dollars needed to purchase all of the needed materials for purchasing the new equipment.

d. A list of material items should be defined in the "Includes" section.

6. The "Total Investment" section is used to record total dollars needed to satisfy the purchase of needed equipment or equipment updates.

TIP #1: The Proposed Investment Expense form should be used only for investments that are similar. For example, if more than one type of equipment will be proposed, each equipment type should have its own form.

TIP #2: If the proposed investment is hiring more employees, the expenses associated with buying additional equipment and material for each new employee will need to be included on the form. If equipment and materials already exist, you will not need to complete the "Equipment Expense" or "Material Expense" sections.

TIP #3: When proposing new equipment purchases, include any literature on the new equipment for upper management to review.

TIP #4: If the new equipment purchase proposal includes any additional warranty or insurance costs, include such costs in the per unit costs recorded in the "Equipment Expense" section. Define what the warranty or insurance costs covers in the "Includes" section.

Project Cost of Quality FORM 23

The Project Cost of Quality form presents the costs associated with performance that falls short of expectations and needs.

Project Cost of Quality

NAME PC Players   DATE March 6

Project Description

There is lost productivity due to outdated computer equipment and the lack of computers for several employees.

Labor Expense

COST/HOUR	X	# OF PEOPLE	X	# HOURS/DAY	=	TOTAL COST/DAY	ANNUALIZED
$ 15.00		6		6		$ 540.00	$ 135,000.00

INCLUDES

Average hourly rate of all employees for time lost sending all word processing to typing pool, or for using mainframe computer, which is slow and cumbersome.

Equipment Expense

COST/HOUR	X	# OF PEOPLE	X	# HOURS/DAY	=	TOTAL COST/DAY	ANNUALIZED
$ 25.00		1		2.5		$ 62.50	$ 15,625.00

INCLUDES

Downtime (delay) on mainframe due to excessive use.

Material Expense

COST/UNIT	X	# OF UNITS/DAY	=	TOTAL COST/DAY	ANNUALIZED
$ 3.00		1		$ 3.00	$ 900.00

INCLUDES

Paper costs for duplicating work and filing ($3.00 per ream of paper).

Total Cost of Quality Expense for 1 Year $ 151,525.00

Comments

Annualized data is based on 250 working days per year.

PROJECT COST OF QUALITY

The cost of poor performance often includes wasted time, poor use of equipment, incomplete work due to employee shortages, and so on. The Project Cost of Quality form helps to spot the financial impact on the organization and can justify improvement activity.

To complete this form, follow the sequence listed below:

1. Record the name of the person, department, or team that is submitting the cost findings and the date of submittal.
2. In the "Project Description" section, include the nature of the costs for which the form will provide dollar values. It is important to describe the nature of the poor performance.
3. In the "Labor Expense" section, calculate what the total labor costs are in regards to non-performance by employees. There are six components in this section.

   a. First, identify the average "Cost/Hour" pay rate.
   b. Record the "# of People" involved with the poor performance.
   c. The "# Hours/Day" section should reflect an average of lost time per day. (You may use the Process Interruption Analysis form, #10, to measure lost time over a period of time.)
   d. The "Total Cost/Day" is the total labor expense on a daily basis.
   e. To calculate the "Annualized" expense, multiply the "Total Cost/Day" figure by 250 days. (This is the average number of workdays in most organizations.)
   f. The "Includes" section should describe how the "Labor Expense" is being realized.

4. The "Equipment Expense" section represents any costs associated with equipment that breaks down or performs at a slow rate, thus preventing employees from being more effective and efficient. This section has six components.

a. Every piece of equipment has some designated "Cost/Hour" expense. Use the cost figure provided by your accounting department.

b. Record the "# of Machines" that are part of the problem as described in the "Project Description" section.

c. The "# Hours/Day" should reflect an average of lost time per day. (You may use the Process Interruption Analysis form, #10, to measure lost time over a period of time.)

d. The "Total Cost/Day" is the total equipment expense on a daily basis.

e. To calculate the "Annualized" expense, multiply the "Total Cost/Day" figure by 250 days. (This is the average number of workdays in most organizations.)

f. The "Includes" section should describe how the "Equipment Expense" is being realized.

5. Any waste of office supplies, such as paper, business forms, pens, and so on, should be recorded in the "Material Expense" section. If there is more than one material type involved, a more detailed sheet can be used to supplement this form. If a separate form is needed, use the same calculations as identified in this section. This section includes five components.

a. The "Cost/Unit" represents the average cost for each material unit wasted.

b. The total material units that are wasted in one work day should be recorded under "# of Units/Day."

c. The "Total Cost/Day" is arrived at by multiplying the "Cost/Unit" number by the "# of Units/Day."

d. To reach an "Annualized" total, multiply the "Total Cost/Day" figure by 250 workdays.

e. The "Includes" section should define what type of material is being measured in the "Material Expense" section.

6. The "Total Cost of Quality Expense for 1 Year" is reached by adding the "Annualized" totals for each section completed.

7. Record in the "Comments" section any information that would further the understanding of this form or its calculations. Also, footnotes could be recorded in this section.

TIP #1: The Project Cost of Quality form should reflect real costs associated with poor performance.

TIP #2: Be sure to use conservative numbers for labor rates, equipment rates, and material costs. Your accounting office should be able to provide you with cost figures that are acceptable for senior management for budget purposes.

TIP #3: Not every section on this form may be applicable for every problem.

TIP #4: Realize that the annualized expense is true only if the problem was not corrected or improved. The annualized costs developed on this form often represent the hidden costs of poor performance results.

TIP #5: If recommended improvement action is taken, this form should be kept on file and compared to future improvements. A future comparison can be made to show the benefits gained by having implemented the solution.

Project Benefits and Savings FORM 24

The Project Benefits and Savings form provides a commentary and cost analysis of the project benefits and savings of implementing a proposed solution.

Project Benefits and Savings

NAME _PC Players_   DATE _March 13_

Project Description

Purchase PCs for every office employee and printers for each department.

Projected Benefits

LABOR
300 employee hours saved per day (50 employees saving an average of 6 hours per workday).
Average compensation is $15.00 per man-hour.

EQUIPMENT
10% increase in speed of mainframe—total value of mainframe in operation.

MATERIALS
20% reduction of paper costs @ $3.00 per ream of paper.

OTHER
25% improvement in accuracy of administrative assistants "regular duties."

Projected Savings

	CURRENT COST	% 1ST YEAR SAVINGS		TOTAL SAVINGS
LABOR	$ 162,000.00	100	%	$ 162,000.00
EQUIPMENT	$ 500,000.00	10	%	$ 50,000.00
MATERIALS	$ 900.00	20	%	$ 180.00
OTHER	$ *		%	$

Explanation *The estimated increase in administrative output was not included in the financial savings.

Total Projected 1st Year Savings $ 212,180.00

Comments

PROJECT BENEFITS AND SAVINGS

The Project Benefits and Savings form ties the previous forms (#22 and #23) together. The calculations completed previously can now be presented as a total savings for the project.

To complete this form, follow the sequence listed below:

1. Record the name of the person, department, or team that is submitting the overview and the date of submittal.
2. In the "Project Description" section, state the intended solution.
3. In the "Projected Benefits" section, address the four areas listed in commentary form.

   a. Describe any benefits to the labor involved with implementing the solution. Use numbers of employees and anticipated time savings.
   b. Any projected improvements for equipment should be recorded.
   c. Projected savings of materials should be noted.
   d. Other savings or benefits can be included in the "Other" section.

4. The "Projected Savings" section makes use of several pieces of information already calculated on previous forms. This section has five components.

   a. Labor's current cost, projected as a percentage of first year savings, and the total savings for the first year, should be recorded.
   b. Equipment's current cost should reflect the annual operating expense for all of the equipment considered part of the project's scope. The projected percentage of first year savings should be recorded, and the total savings should reflect a monetary amount.
   c. The current cost of materials, with projected percentage of first year savings and total savings, should be recorded.

d. The "Other" section provides an area for any other costs that needed to be represented. (This area could be used for second equipment calculations or additional material costs.)

e. For any item that is included in the "Other" section, a brief description can be made in the "Explanation" section.

5. The "Total Projected 1st Year Savings" is simply the total savings for the labor, equipment, material, and other costs.

6. General summary comments should be recorded in the appropriate section.

TIP #1: Combined with the Project Overview form (#21), the Projected Benefits and Savings form provides a brief and informative review of what is being requested.

TIP #2: Keep the percentages used in the "Projected Benefits" section realistic and conservative.

TIP #3: Attach any documentation to this form that supports each of the cost areas identified.

Project Return on Investment FORM 25

The Project Return on Investment form can be used to calculate the percentage return that should be realized on an initial investment to implement a proposed solution.

Project Return on Investment

NAME PC Players   DATE March 20

Project Description

PC Players request the purchase of PCs for every office employee and laser printers for
each department. This will increase productivity of all employees, free up administrative
assistants, and decrease the workload on the mainframe computer.

$$\text{ROI} = \frac{\text{Total Investment}}{\text{1st Year Savings}} = \text{Payback in Years}$$

$$\text{ROI} = \frac{\$\ 91,700.00}{\$\ 212,180.00} = \frac{.43}{} \text{ Payback in Years}$$

Comments

The investment will be realized in 5.16 months (.43 x 12) after purchasing the PCs.

PROJECT RETURN ON INVESTMENT

Most business decisions to purchase equipment or add employees often consider the return on investment (ROI). For example, if a $50,000 investment in new computers could generate more than the same amount in improvements and performance increases, then such a positive return on the original $50,000 might justify the decision to buy the equipment. Remember, a return on investment simply projects how much of the initial investment will be returned within a period of time.

To complete this form, follow the sequence listed below:

1. Record the name of the person, department, or team that is submitting the projected Project Return on Investment form and the date of submittal.
2. In the "Project Description" section, include the primary purpose of the project and the proposed investment request.
3. The ROI is calculated by dividing the total investment (costs) by the 1st year savings (See form #22). The ROI is shown as a payback in years for realizing the investment.

TIP #1: Use the Project Return on Investment form to help influence senior management's decision to invest money to support a solution.

TIP #2: Remember, even with a position ROI, be sure to consider the risk factor involved with implementing the project and/or decision.